Thomas
and the
Jet Plane

THOMAS & FRIENDS

phoenix international publications, inc.

Thomas loves being a tank engine! He loves having wheels and a whistle. And he loves working on the railway.

At the airport, Thomas picks up children for a party. Jeremy the jet plane tells Thomas how wonderful it is to fly.

Being a tank engine doesn't feel as special now.

Thomas chugs away. While he waits for a signal to change, Jeremy flies overhead. Jet planes don't have to stop at signals.

When Thomas stops for a cow on the tracks, Jeremy zooms on by. Jet planes don't have to stop for cows.

At the junction, Thomas stops to let Henry pass. Jeremy flies farther away. Jet planes don't have to stop for freight trains.

Thomas stops for a bridge repair as Jeremy soars into the distance.

"Jet planes can go wherever they like," Thomas grumbles. "Nothing ever stops them."

At last, Thomas arrives at the party.
"I wish I were a jet plane," he says to Percy.
"But engines are Really Useful!" Percy
peeps. Thomas isn't so sure.

Thomas leaves for his next job. Suddenly Jeremy calls over, "A storm's on the way, but I can't warn Sir Topham Hatt — there's nowhere for me to land at the party!"

"This is a job for an engine!" Thomas peeps importantly. He rushes back and loads up the children. Then an idea flies into his funnel!